ISBN-13;978-1542784813
ISBN-10:154278989818
Printed in The United States of America

Welcome to the Letter R Gallery. These pages can be colored with any choice of medium. Colored pencils, watercolor pencils, or your favorite markers can be used. If you use markers or watercolor pencils place a scrap paper under the page you are coloring on.

One artist, Peggy Louise Parrish hand designed all these letters. She included many examples of ways to color them. The possibilities are nearly endless depending on the way you color them. Her colorized gallery selection in each of her letter books are to give ideas. You may copy her examples or choose your own colors.

You are in charge of dressing up these letter Rs with color. If you want to print up any of your colored letters on card stock you may. Please only use these letters for yourself or gifts. Do not sell any of your prints once you have colored them. On card stock these colored letters can be embellished with sparkles and paper crafting. Leave her initials if you make a few "in house" copies for varied choices of coloring.

The Ravishing Letter R

Coloring Book

By Artist Peggy Louise Parrish

C. 2017

Welcome to the Ravishing Letter R

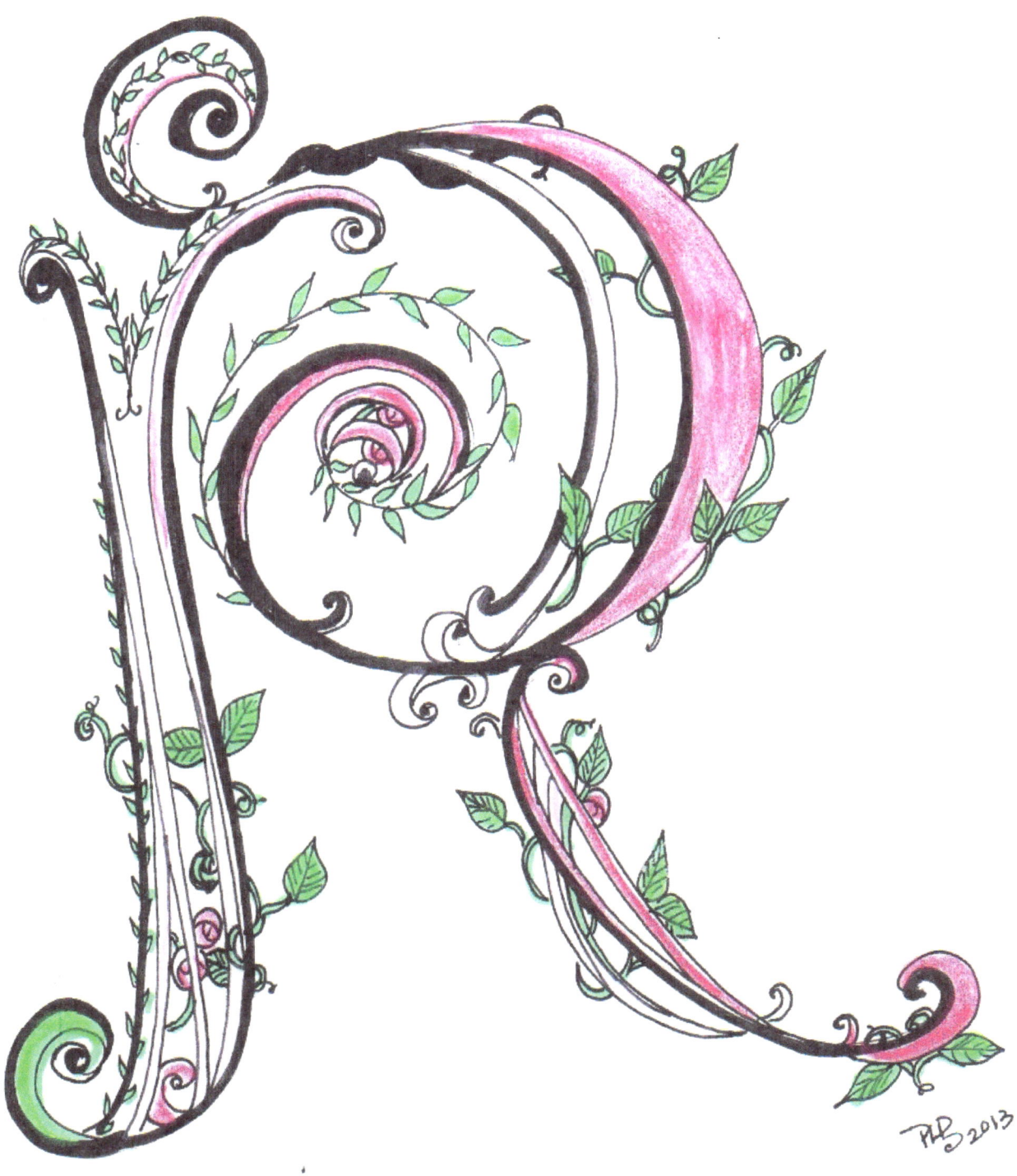

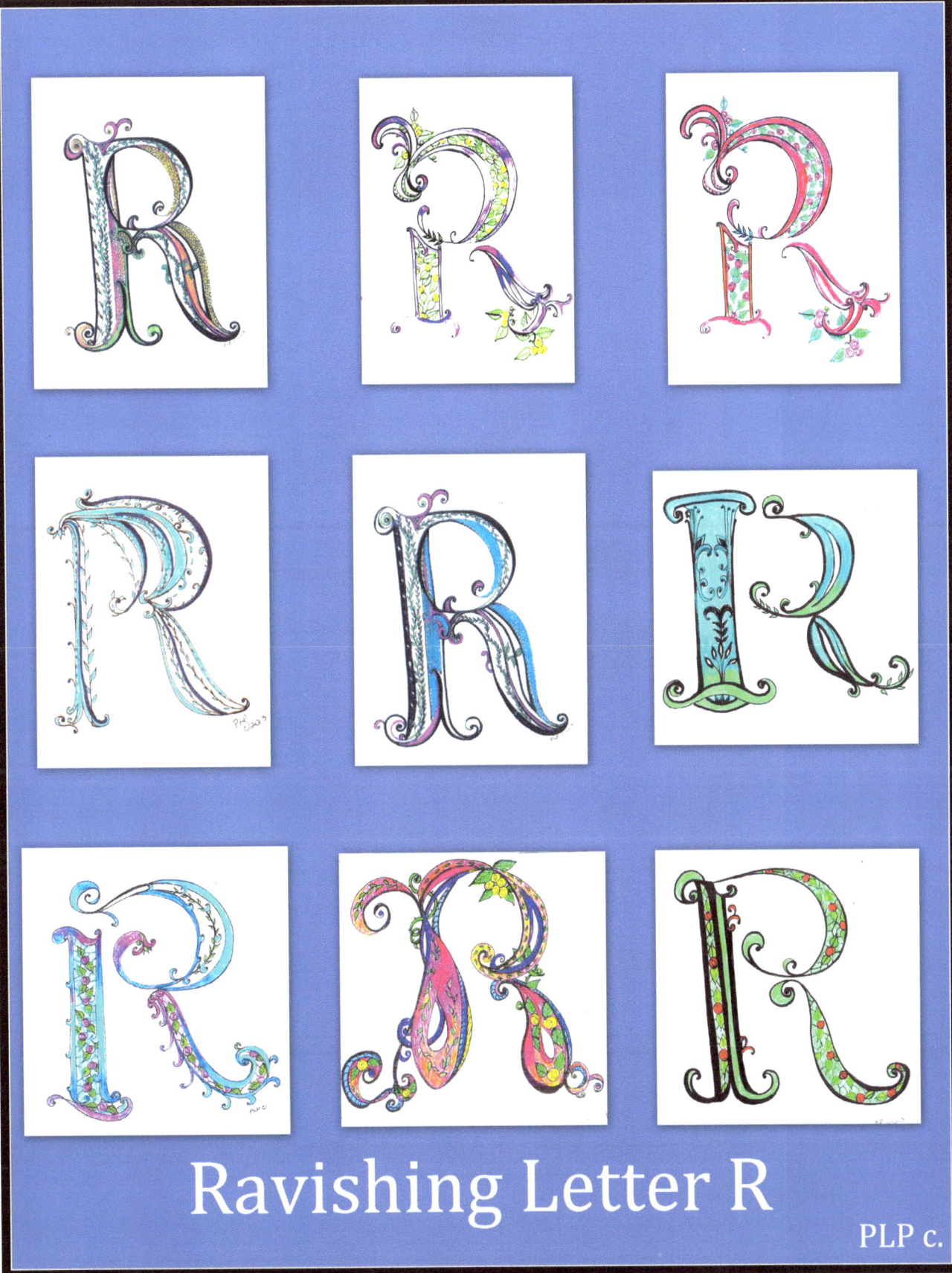

Ravishing Letter R

PLP c.

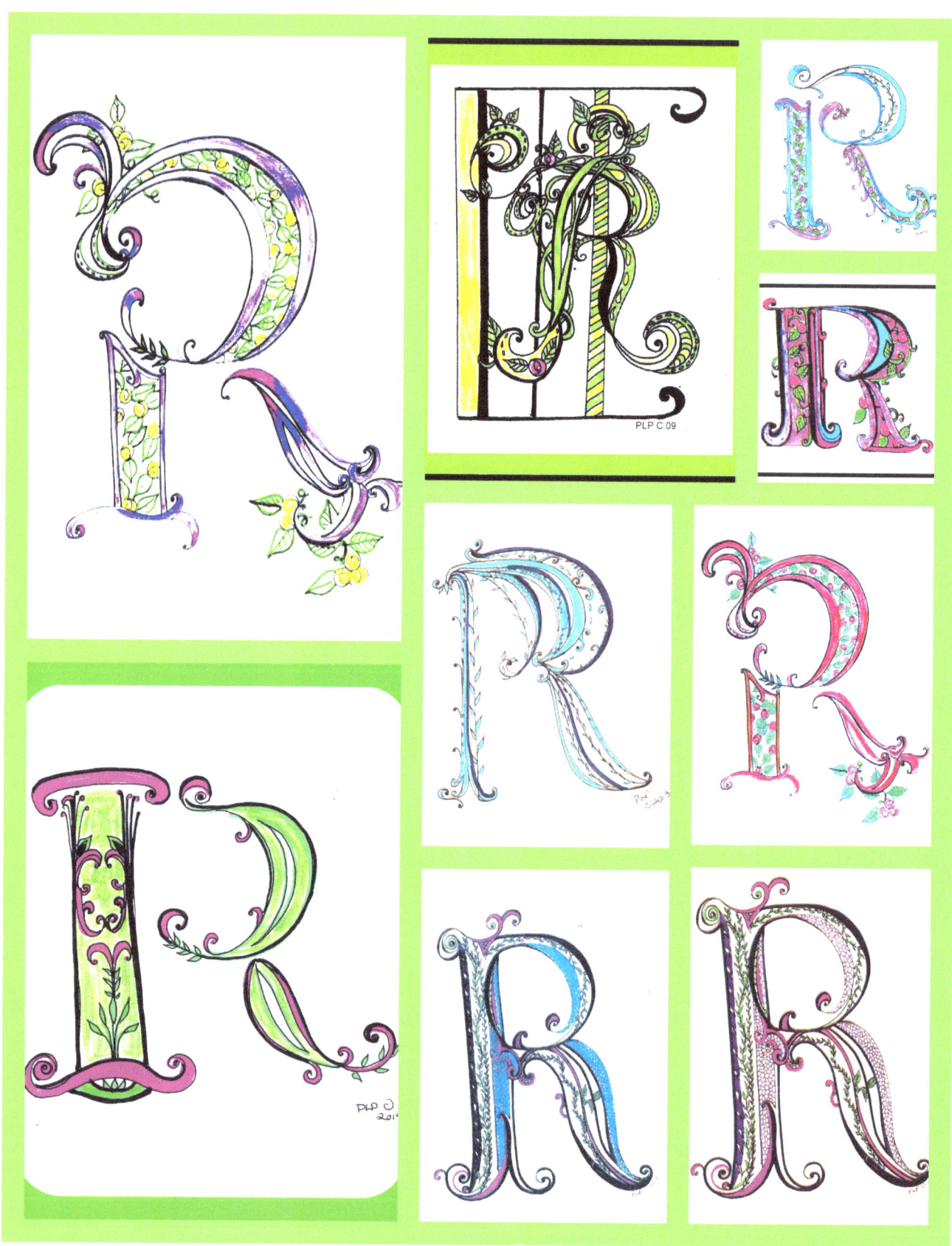

PLP C.09

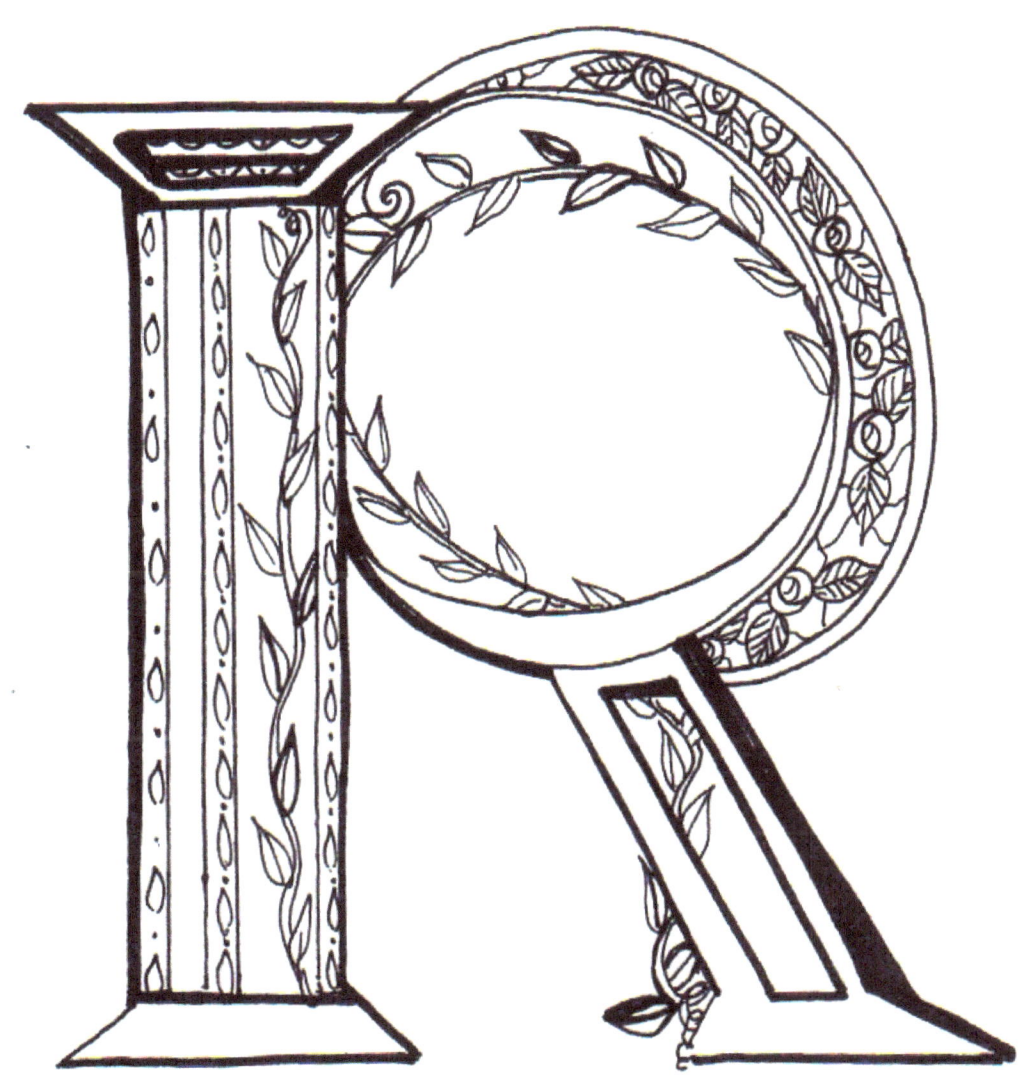

PLP©2010

11

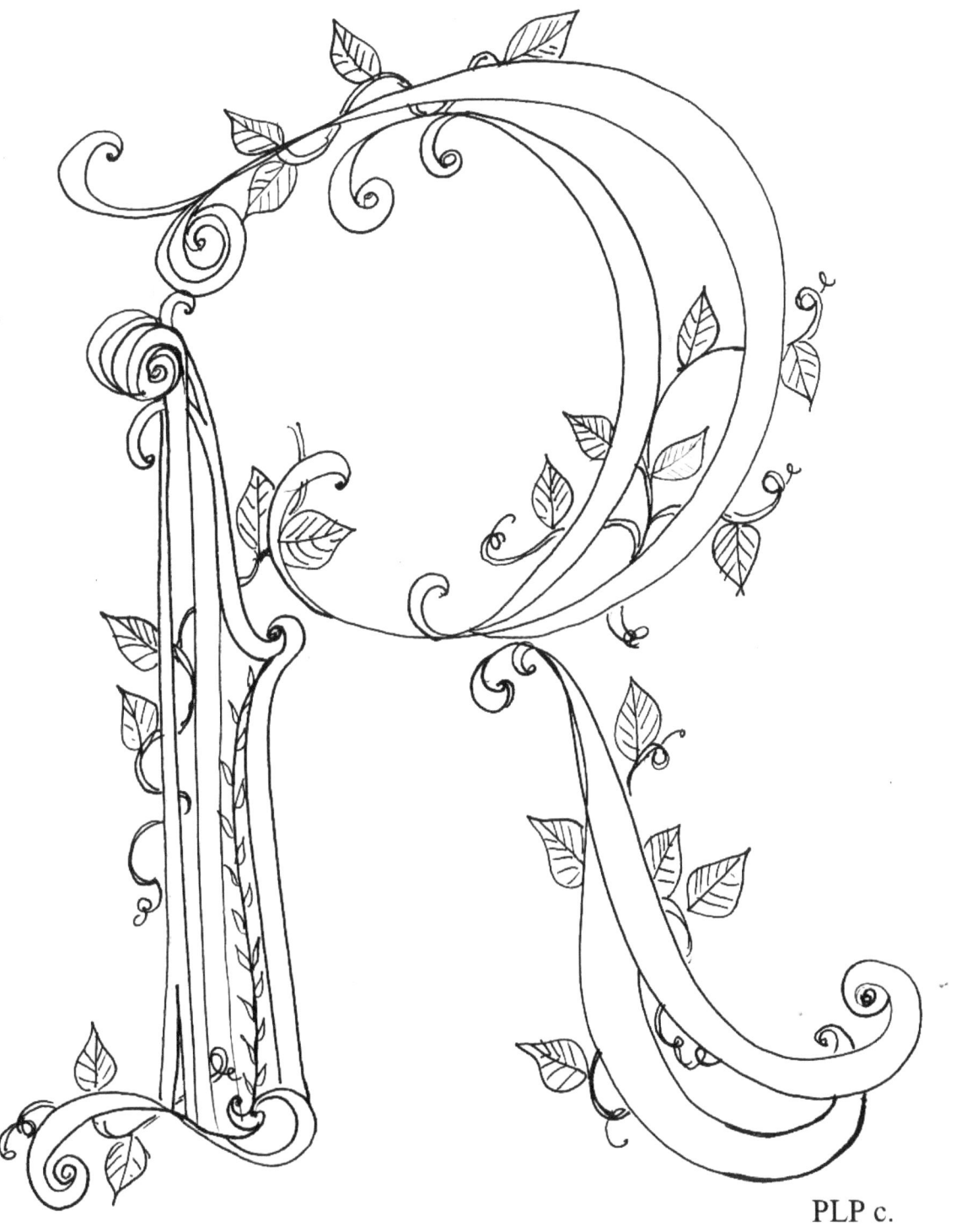

PLP c.

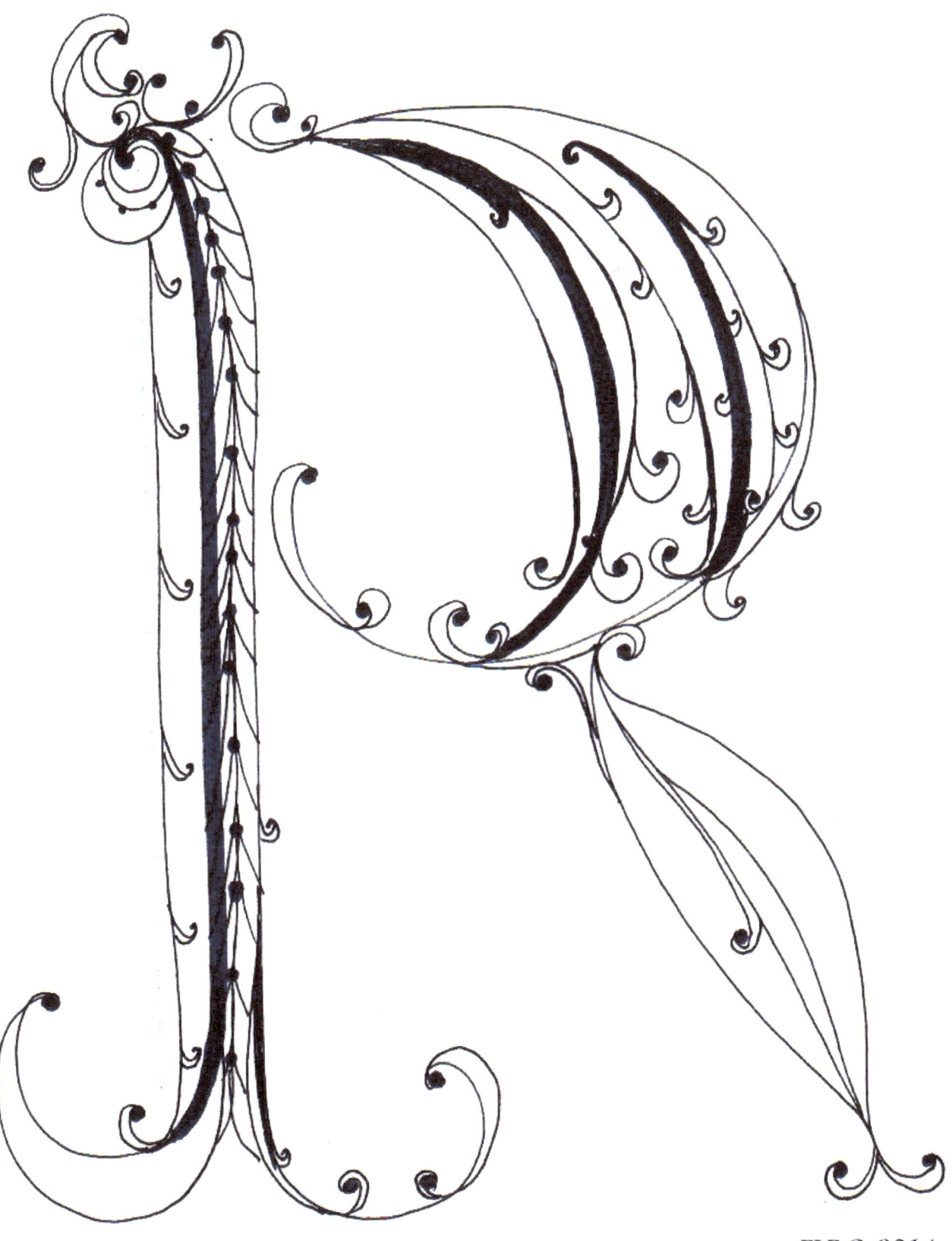

PLP C. 2014

15

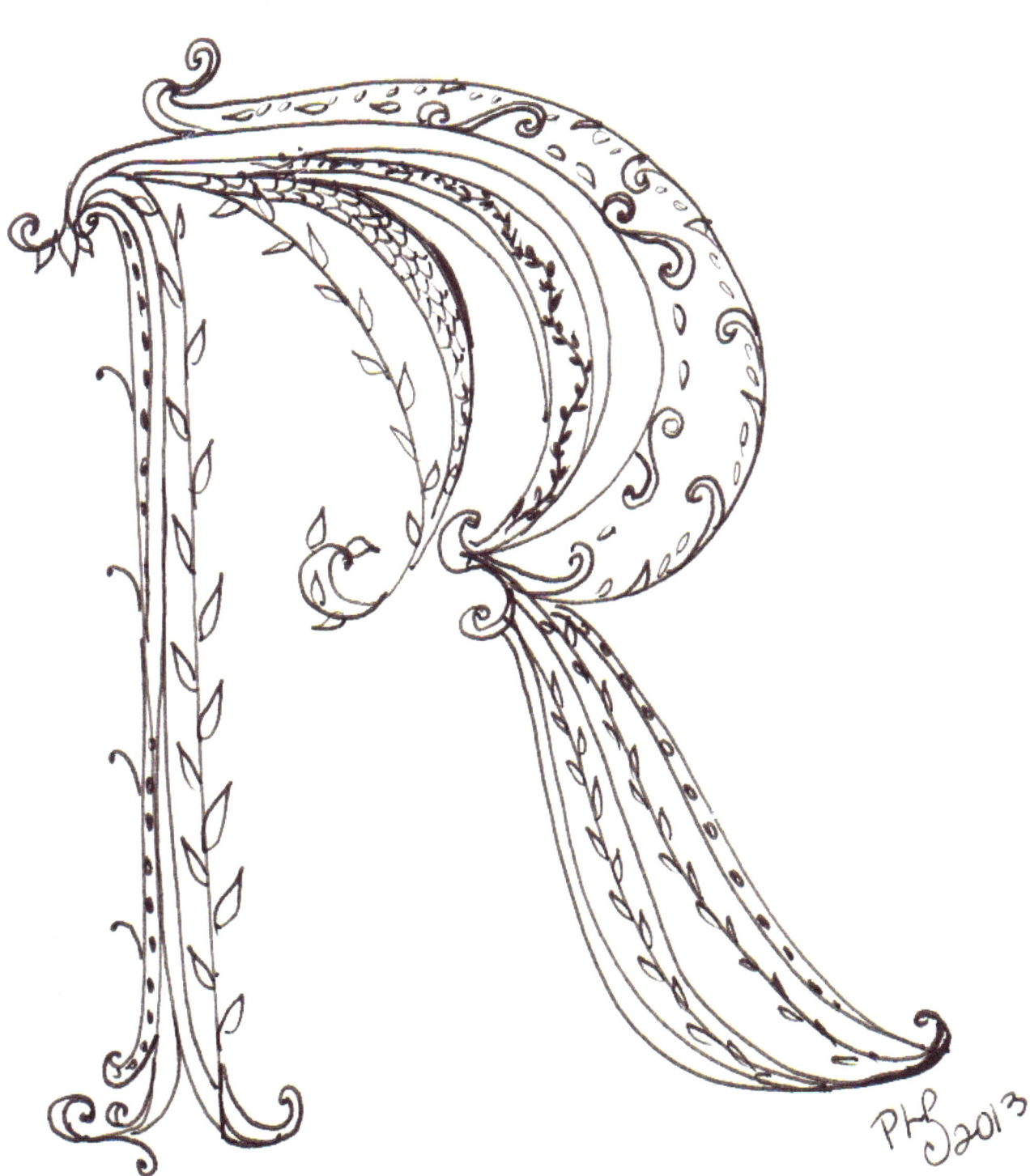

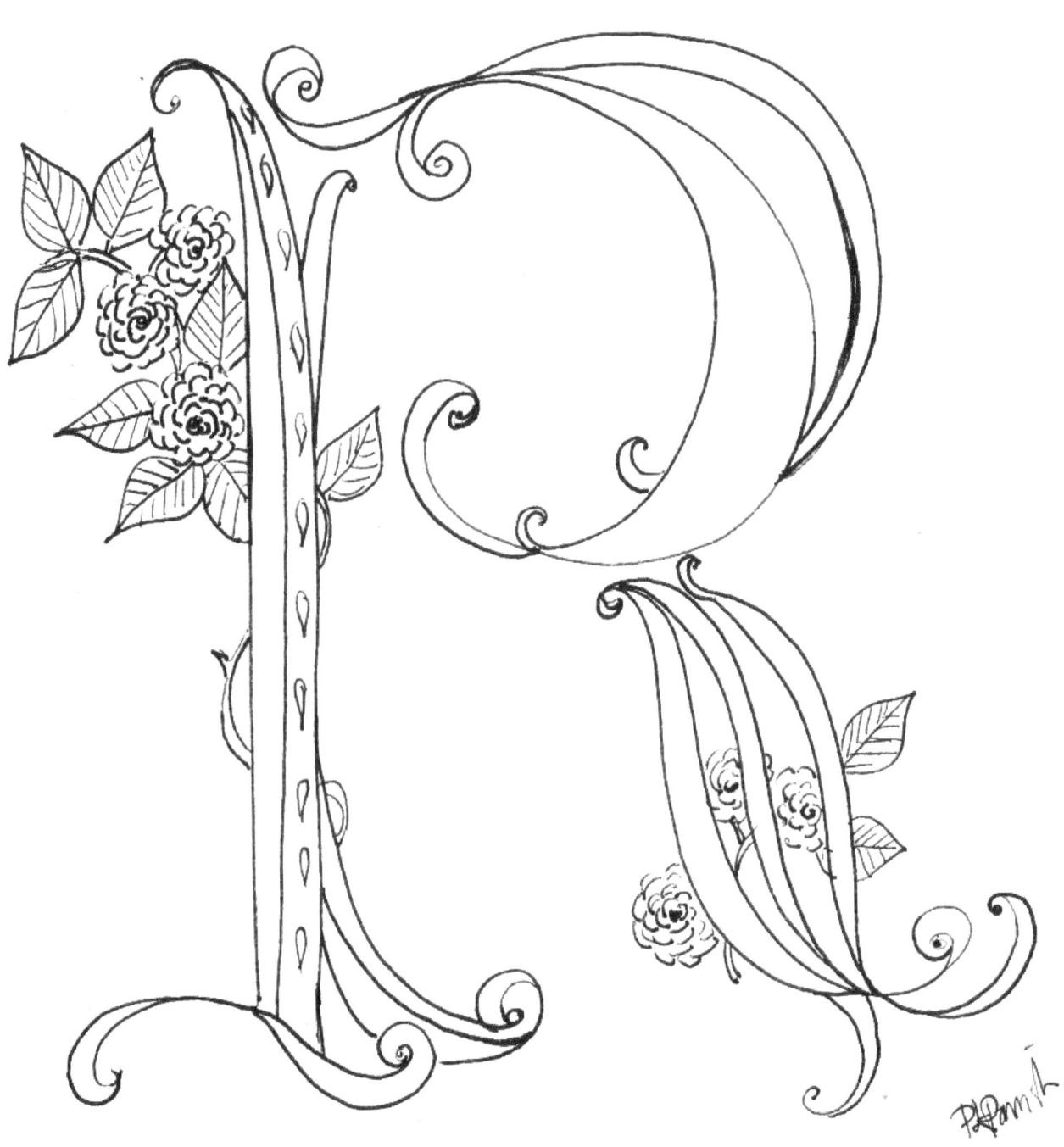

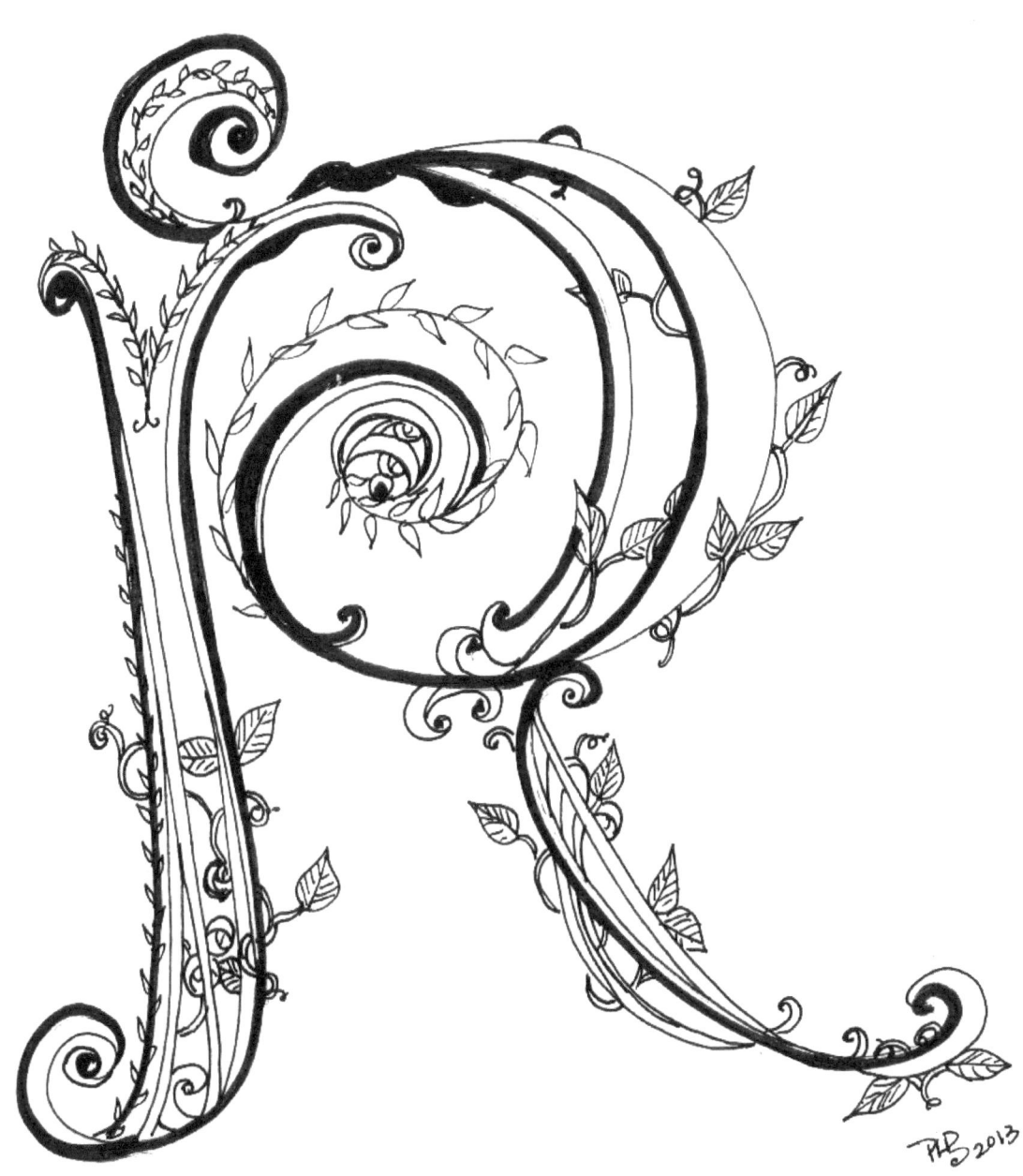

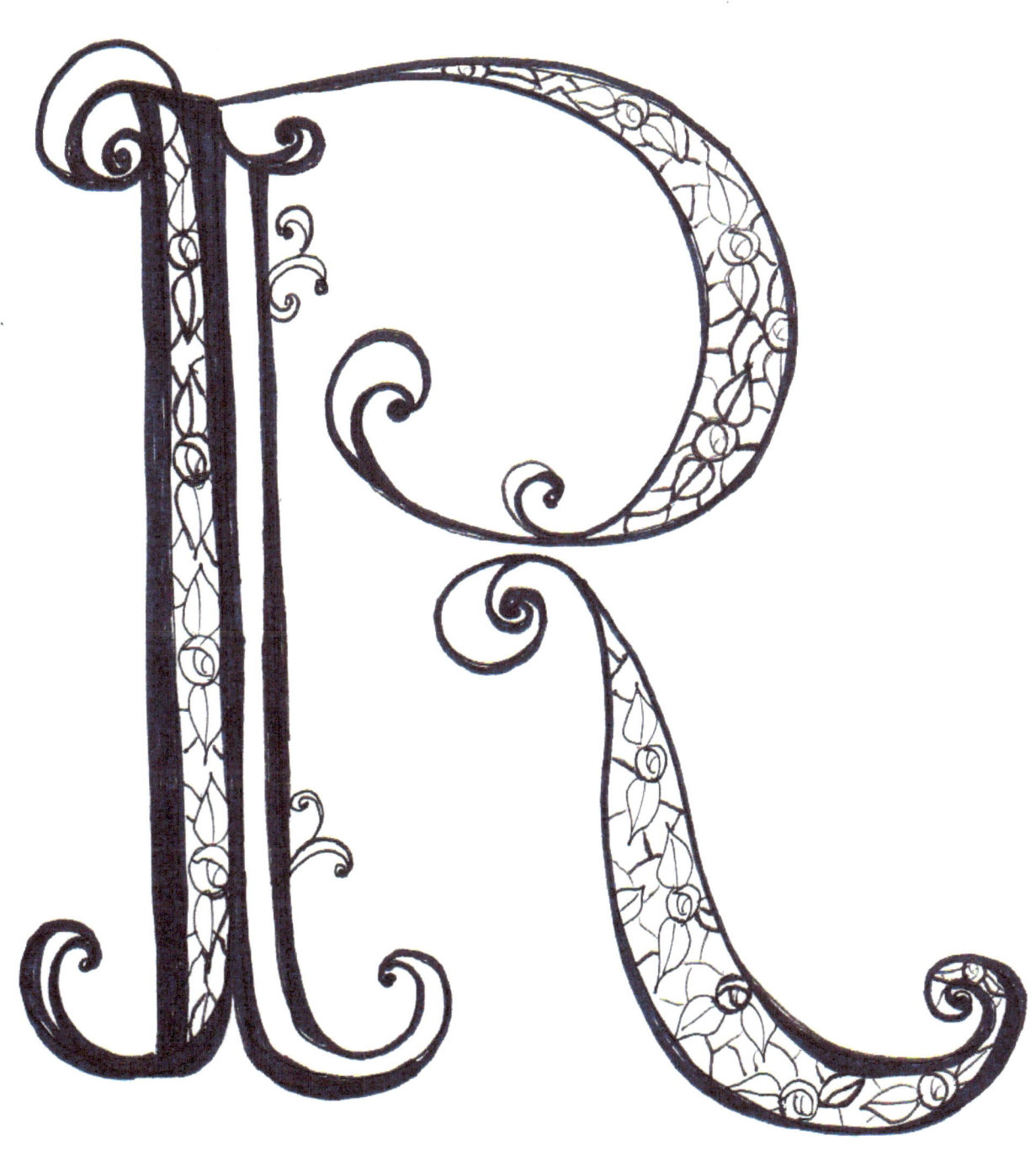

PLP ♄2013

23

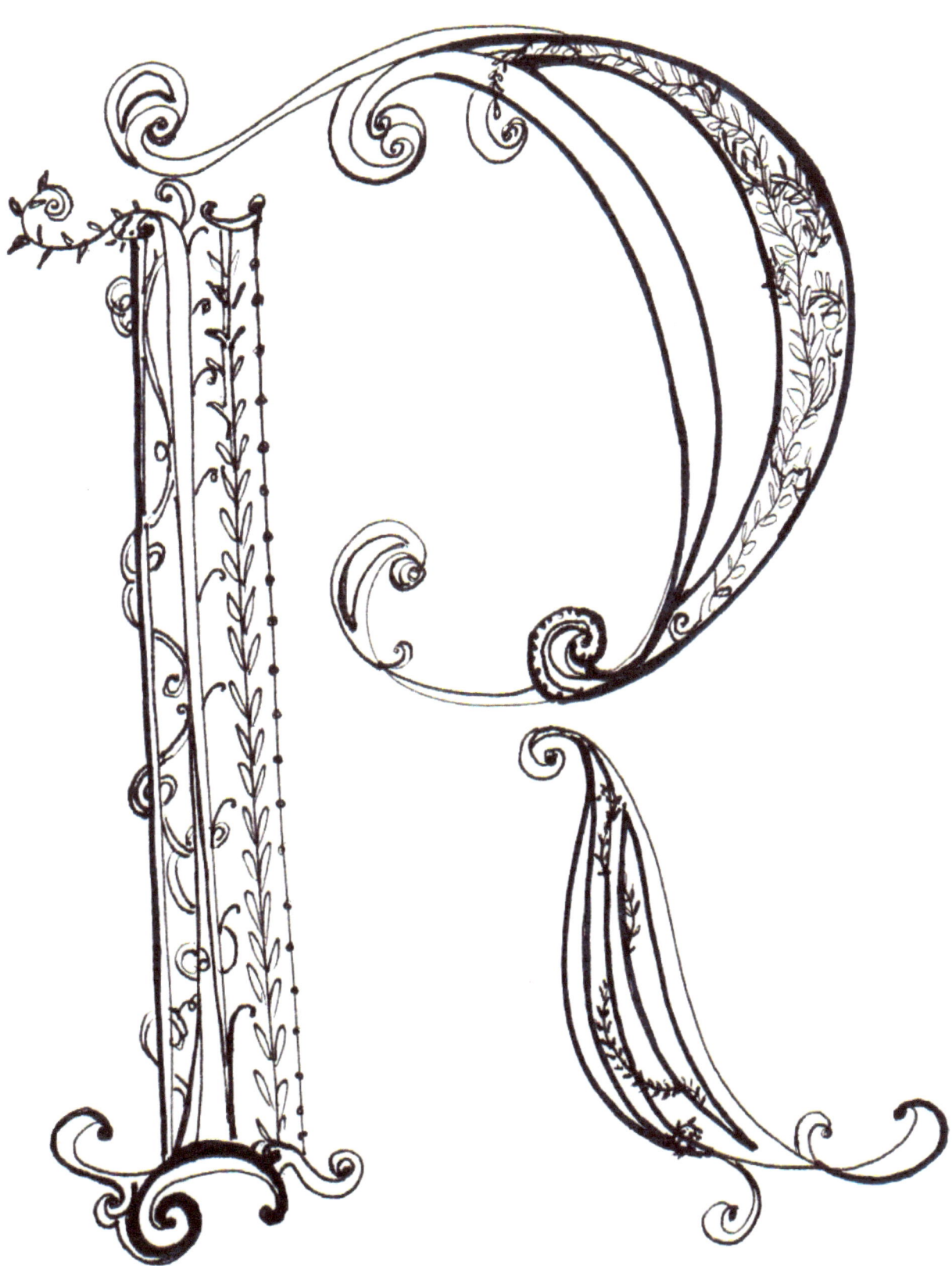

PLD
2013

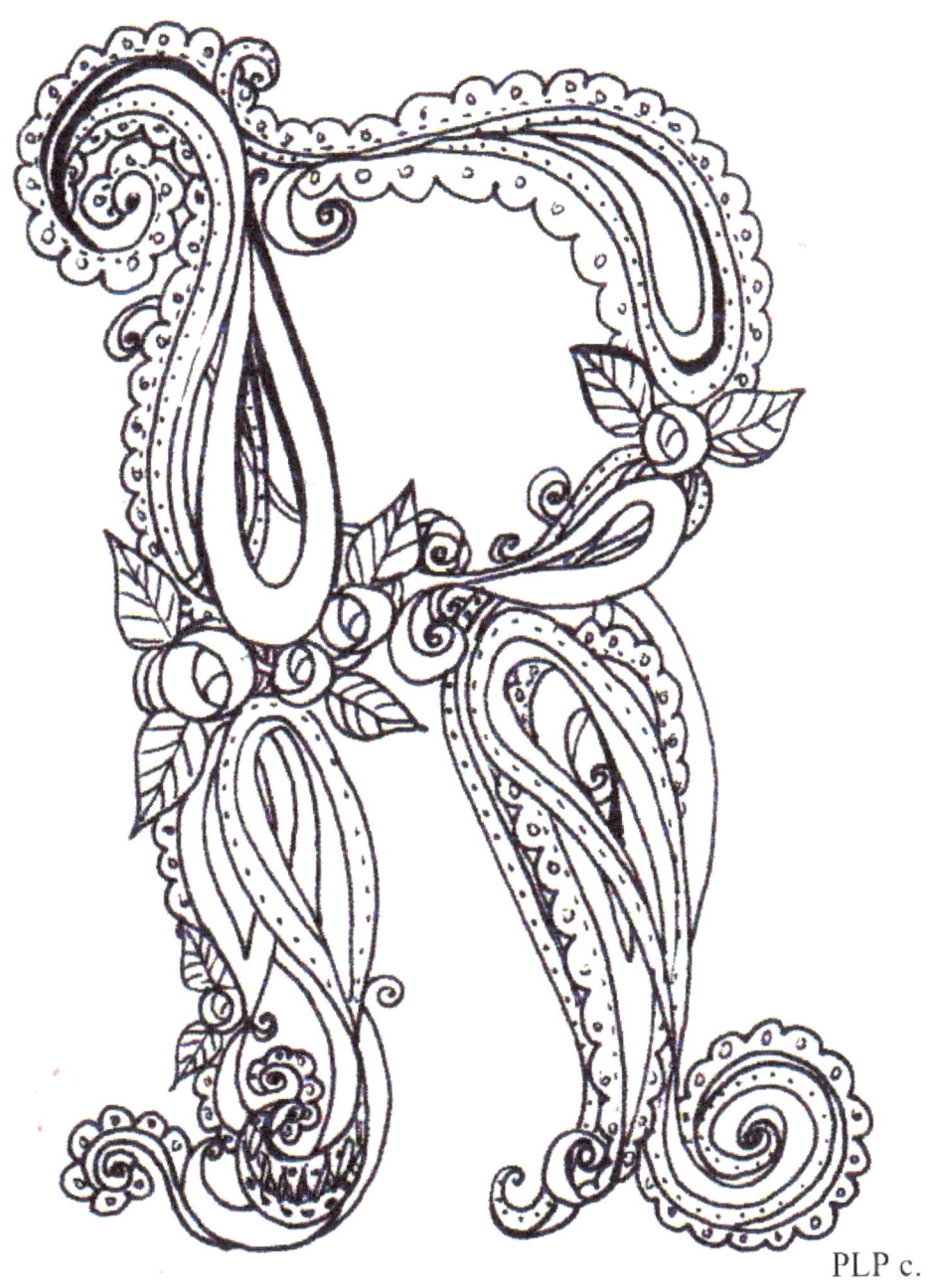

PLP c.

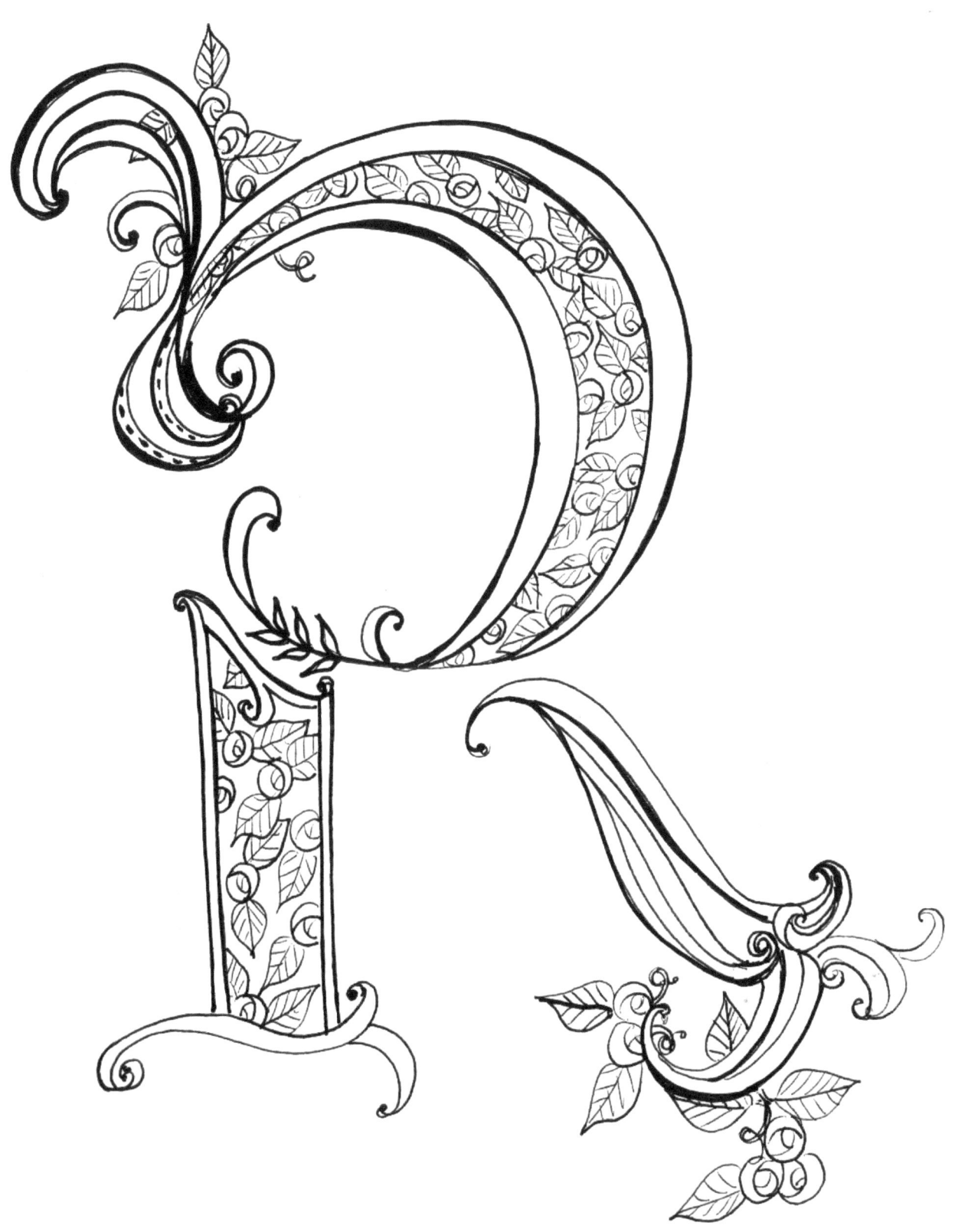

DParrish 09

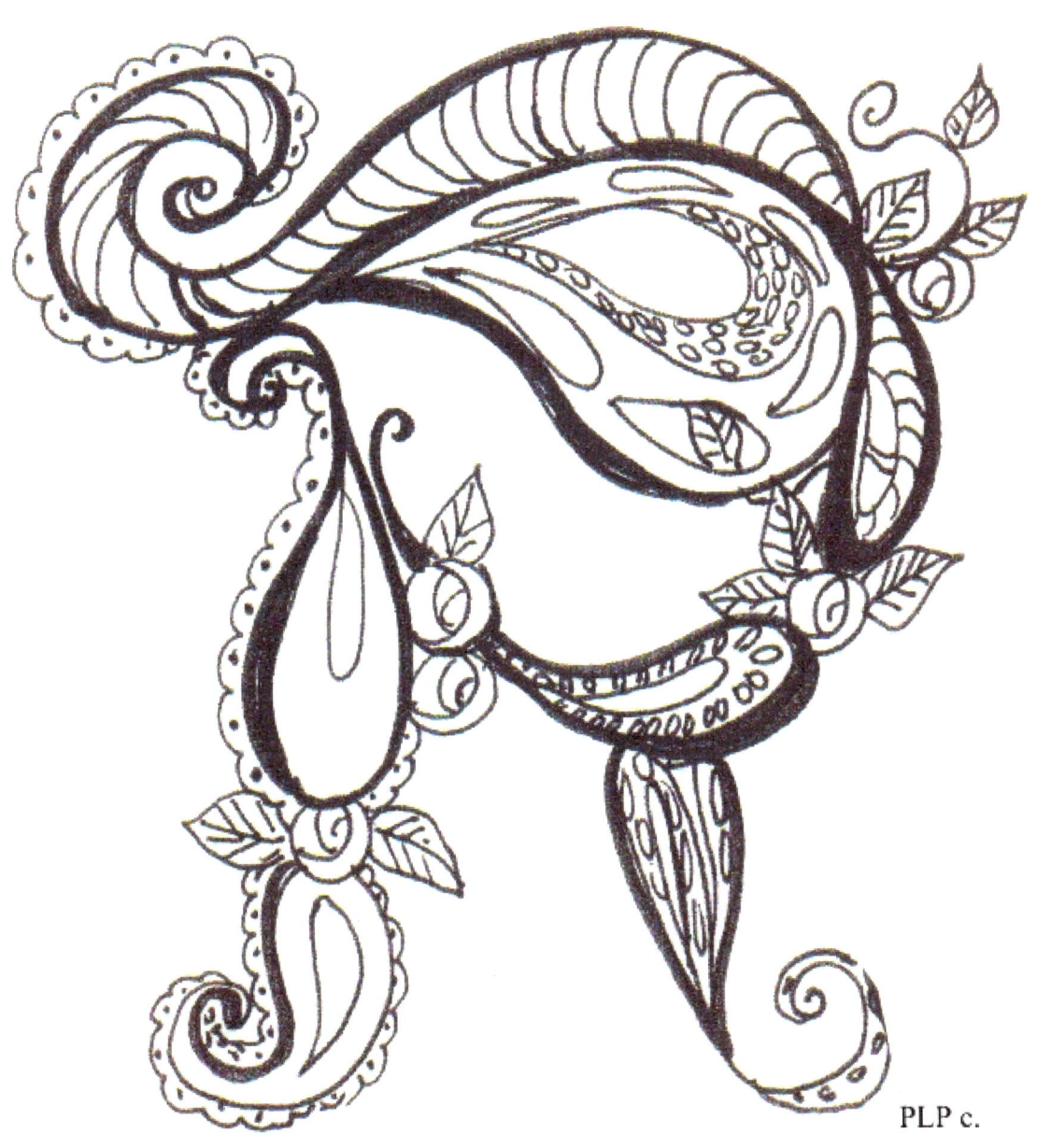

PLP c.

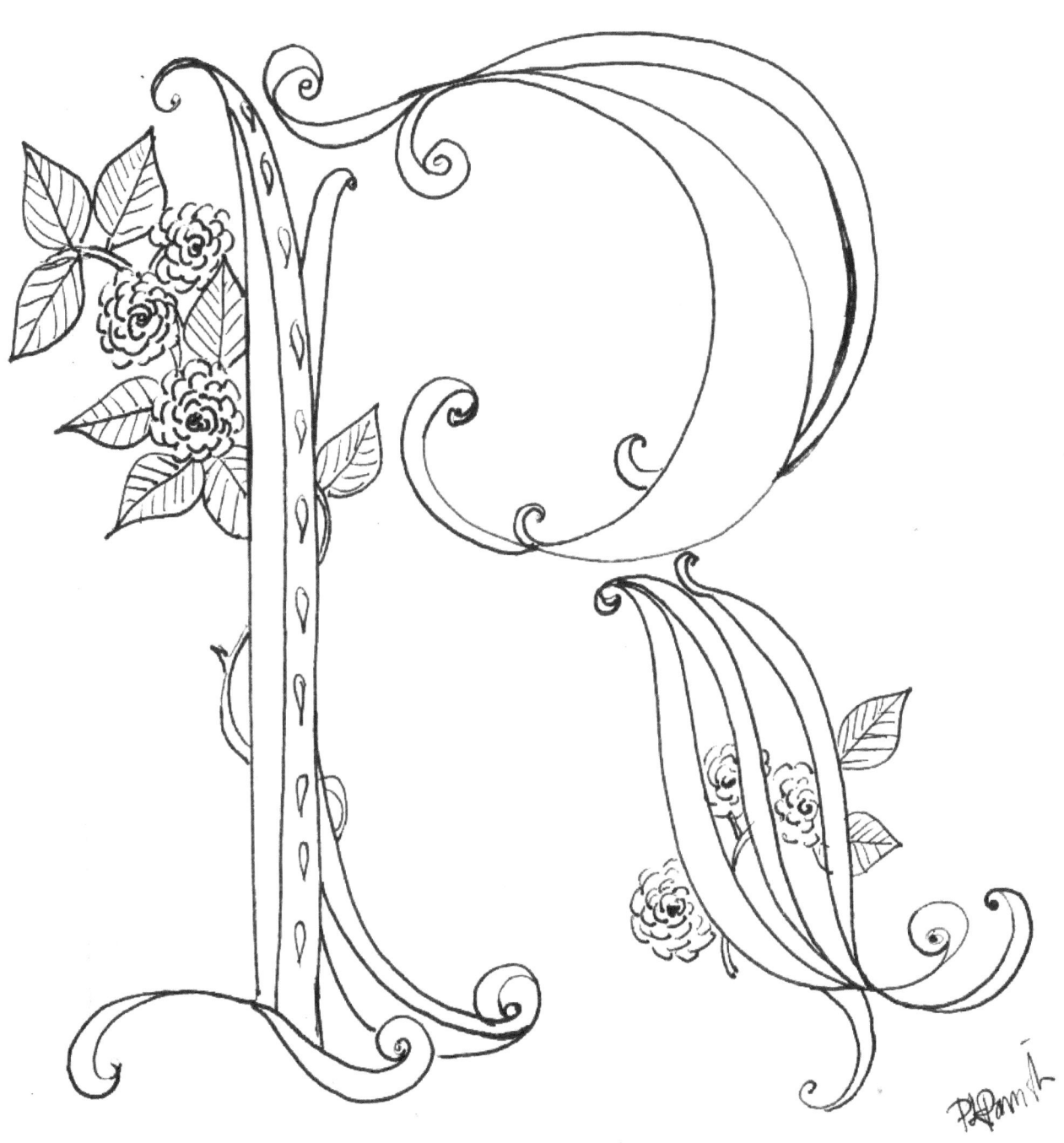

35

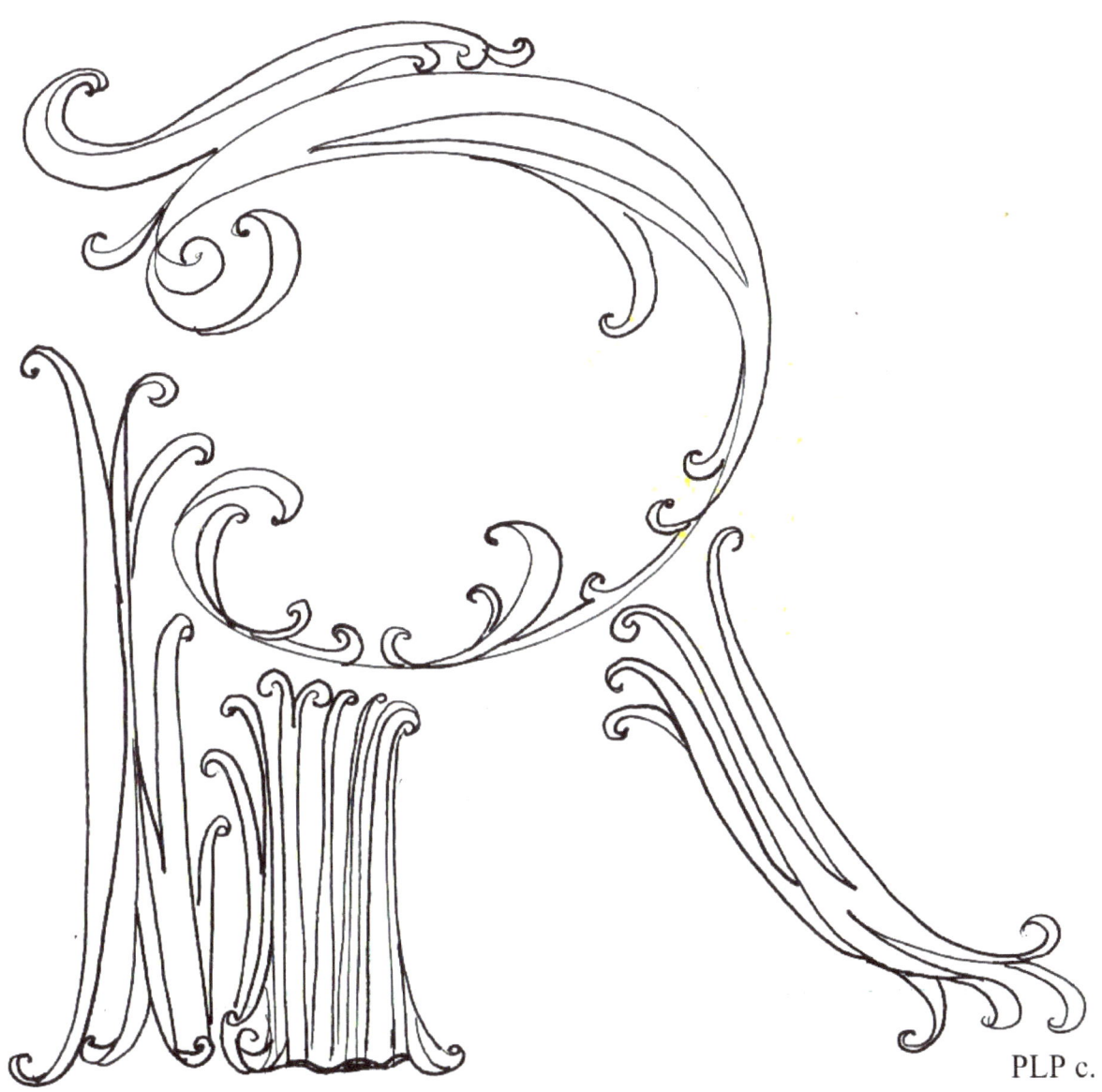

PLP c.

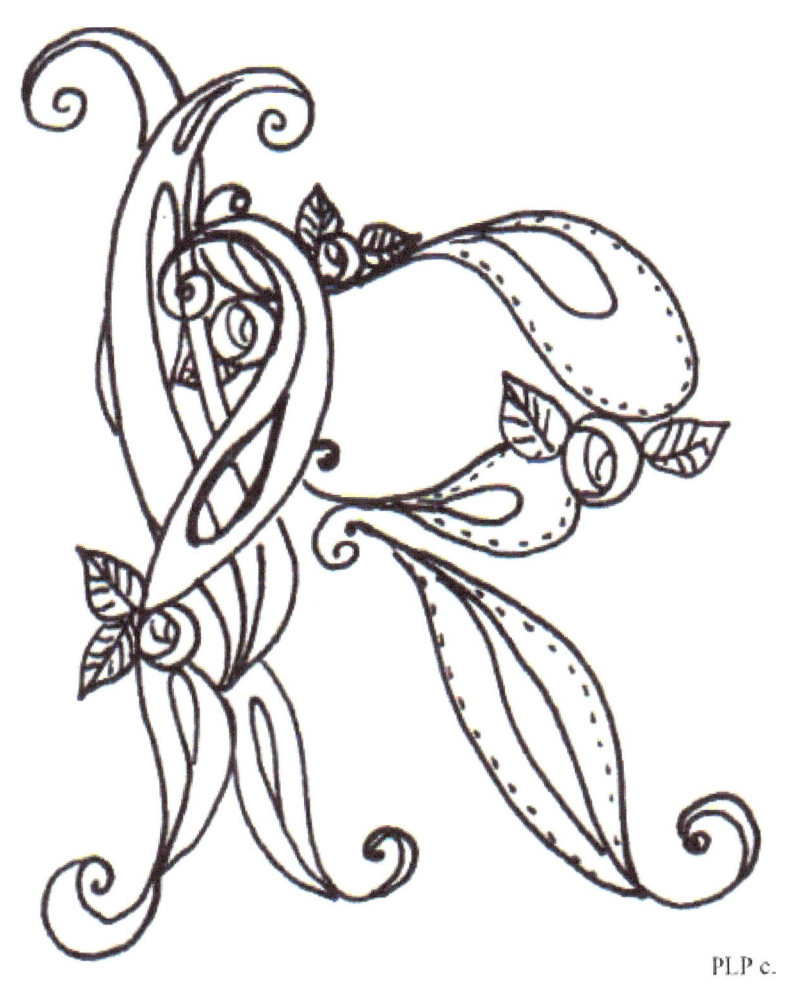

PLP c.

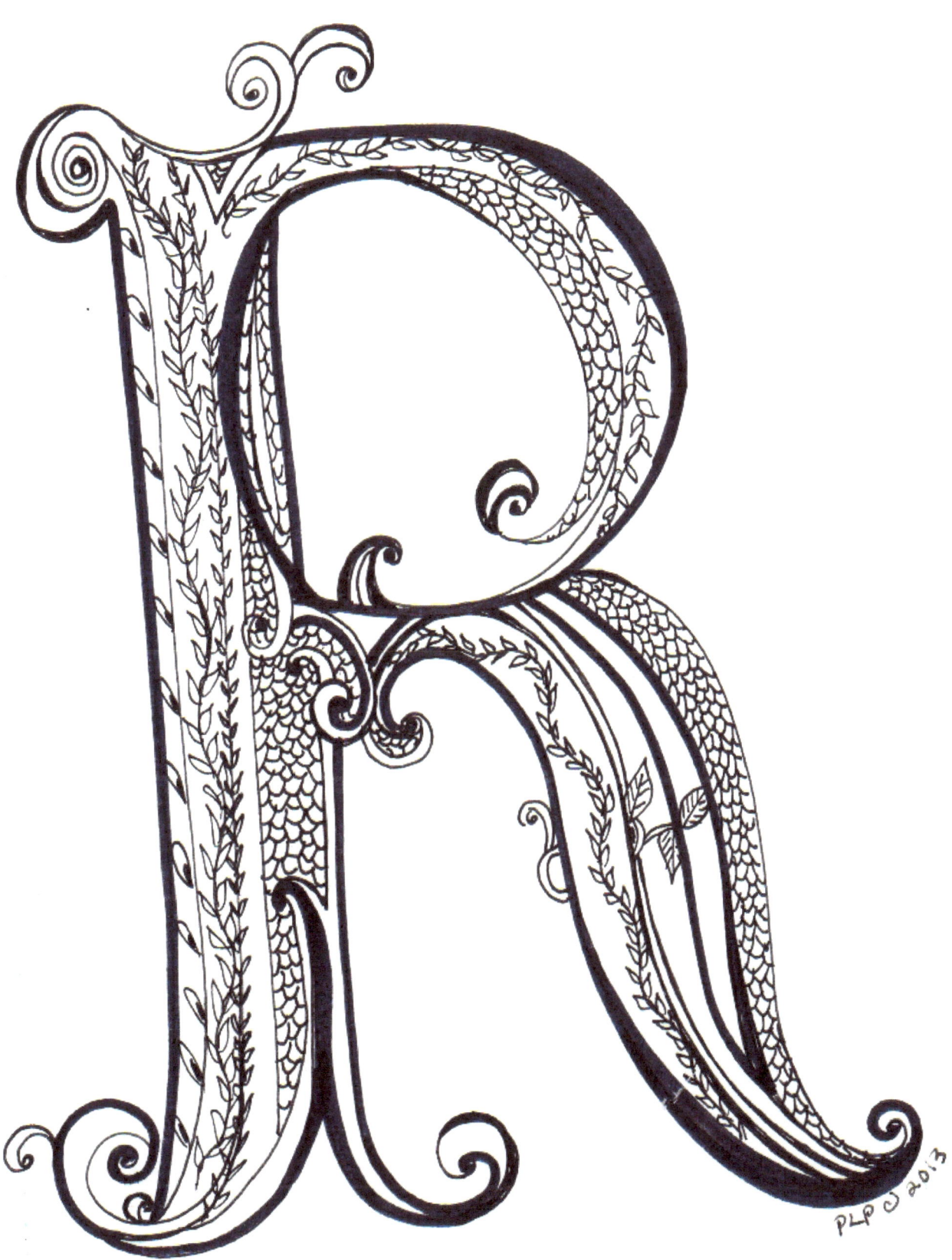

41

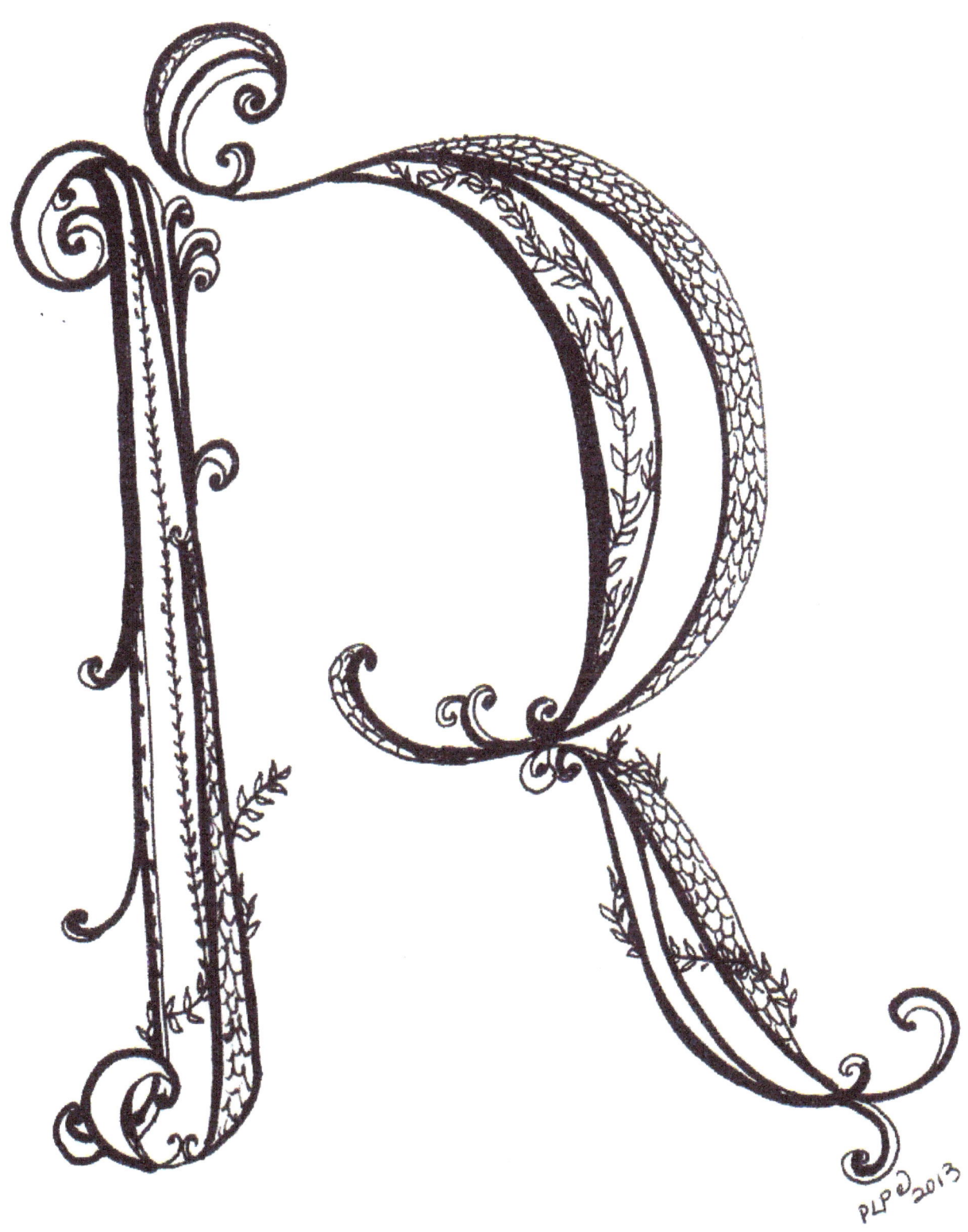

PLP© 2013

43

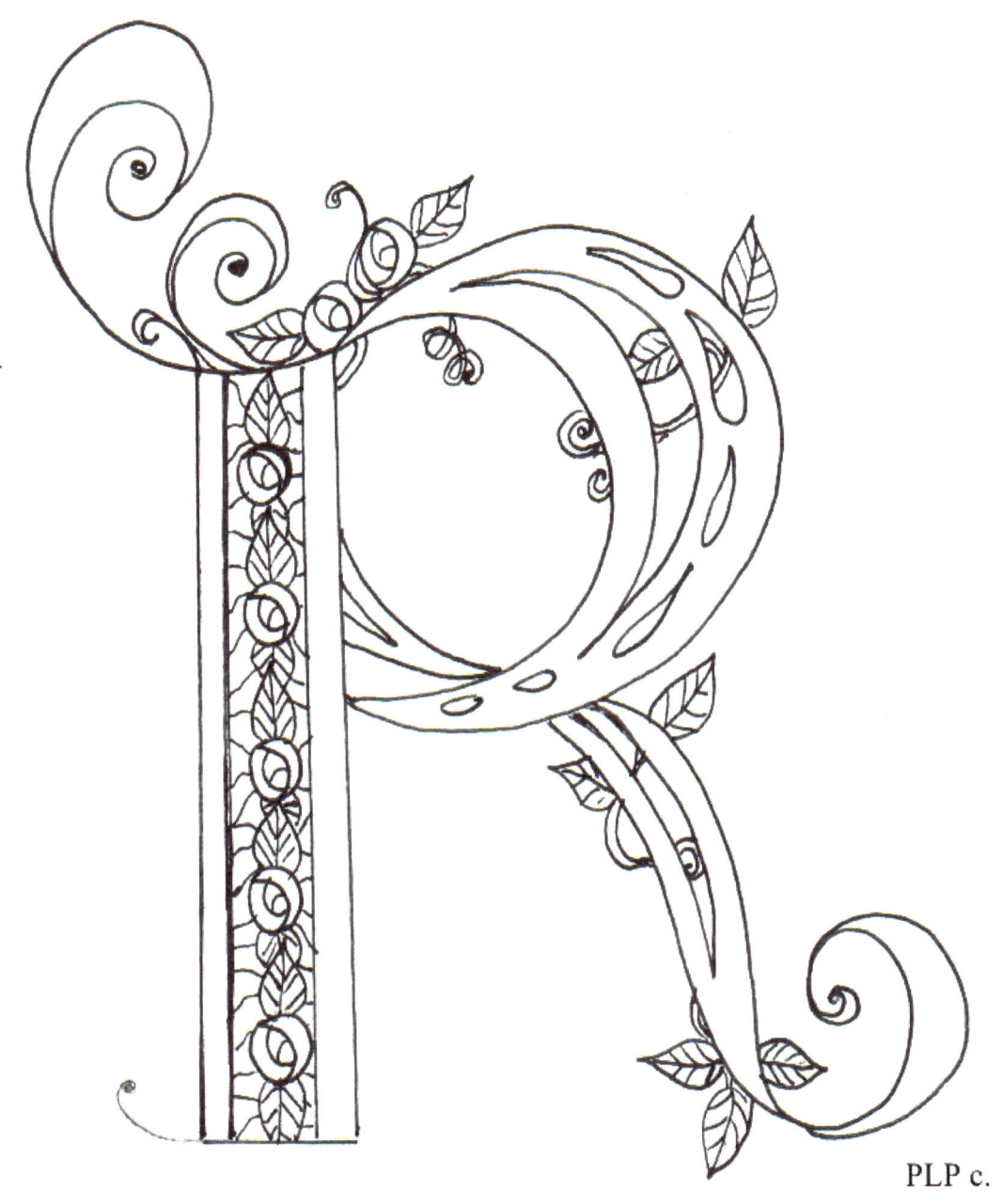

PLP c.

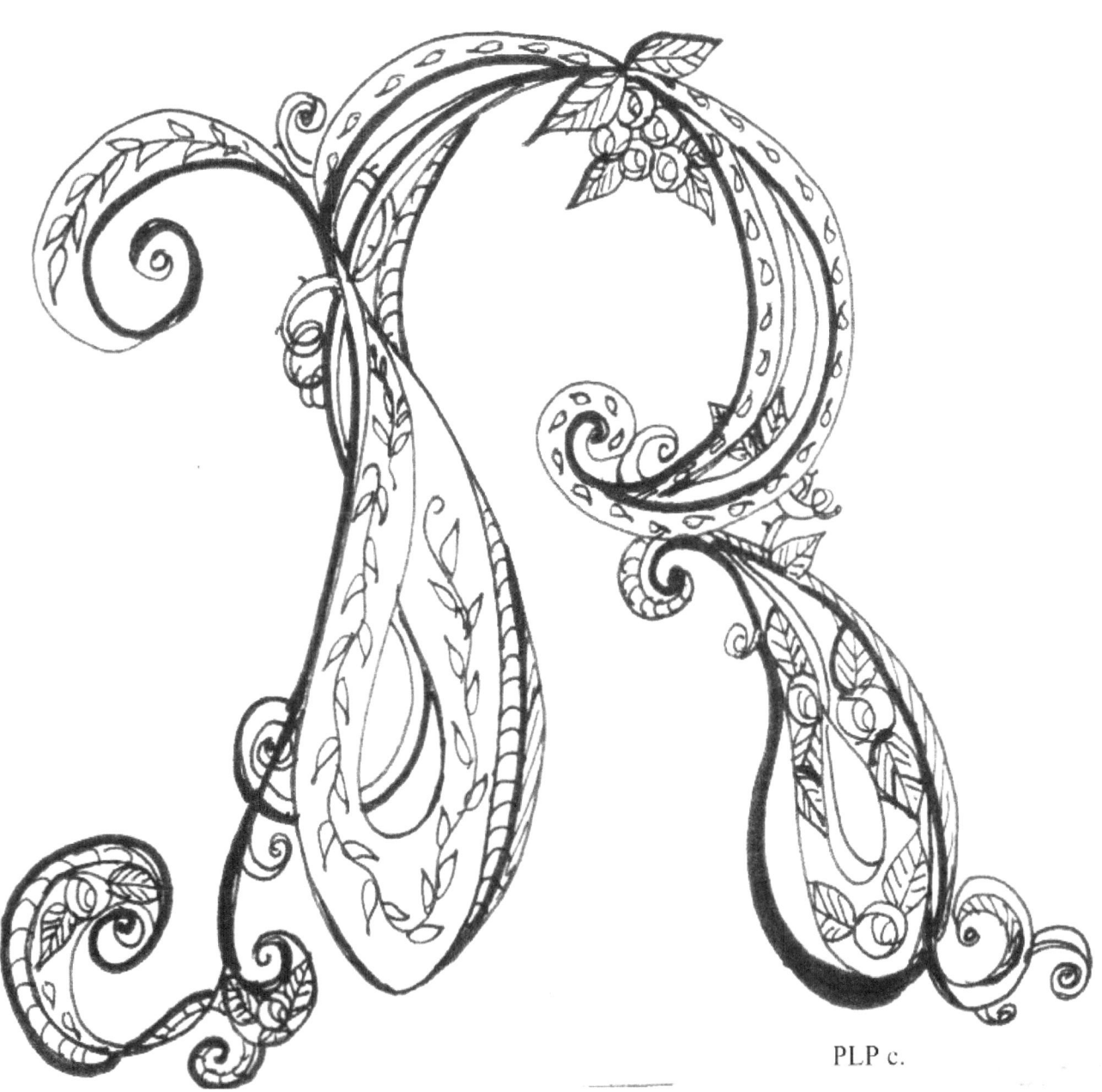

PLP c.

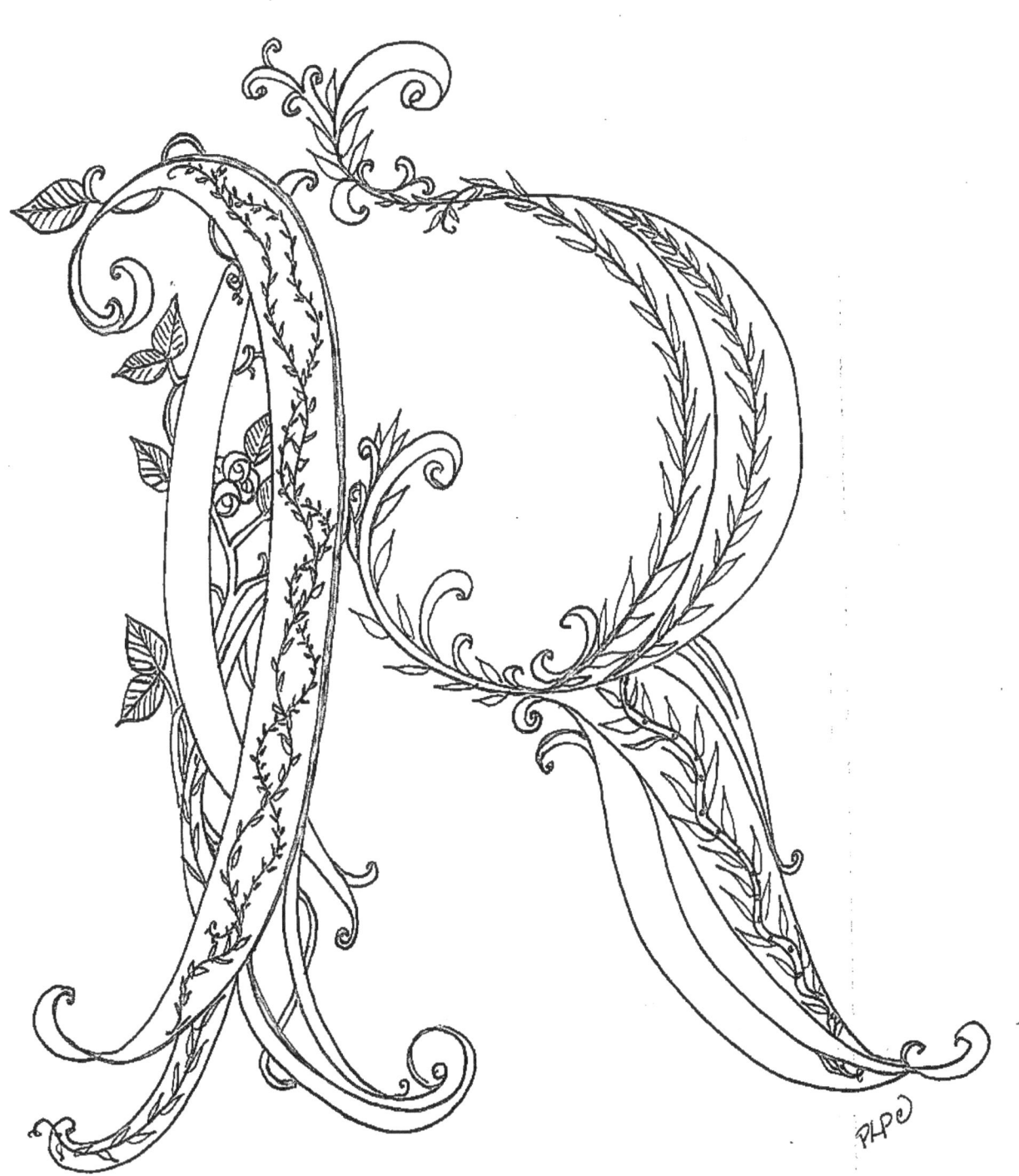

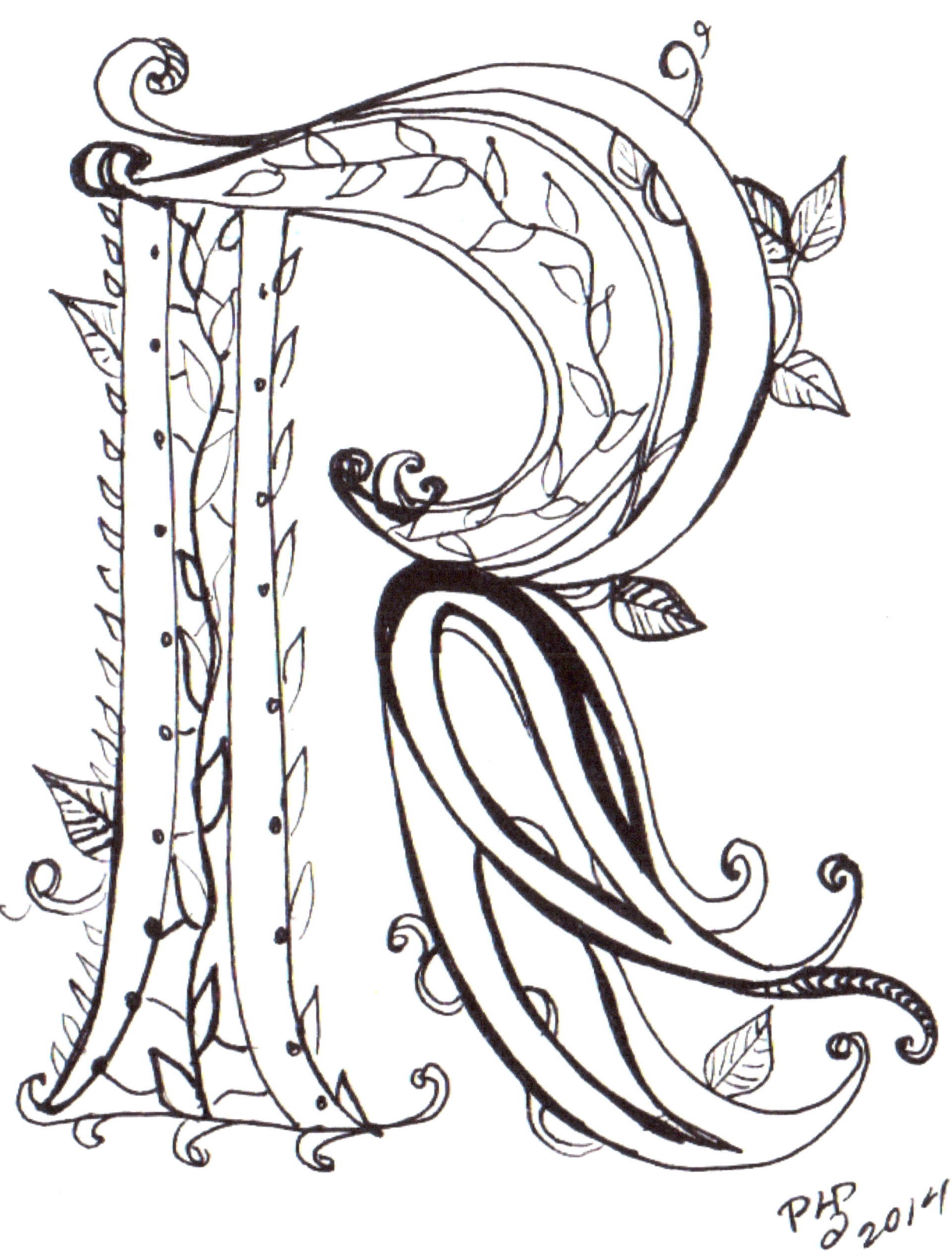

PHB 2014

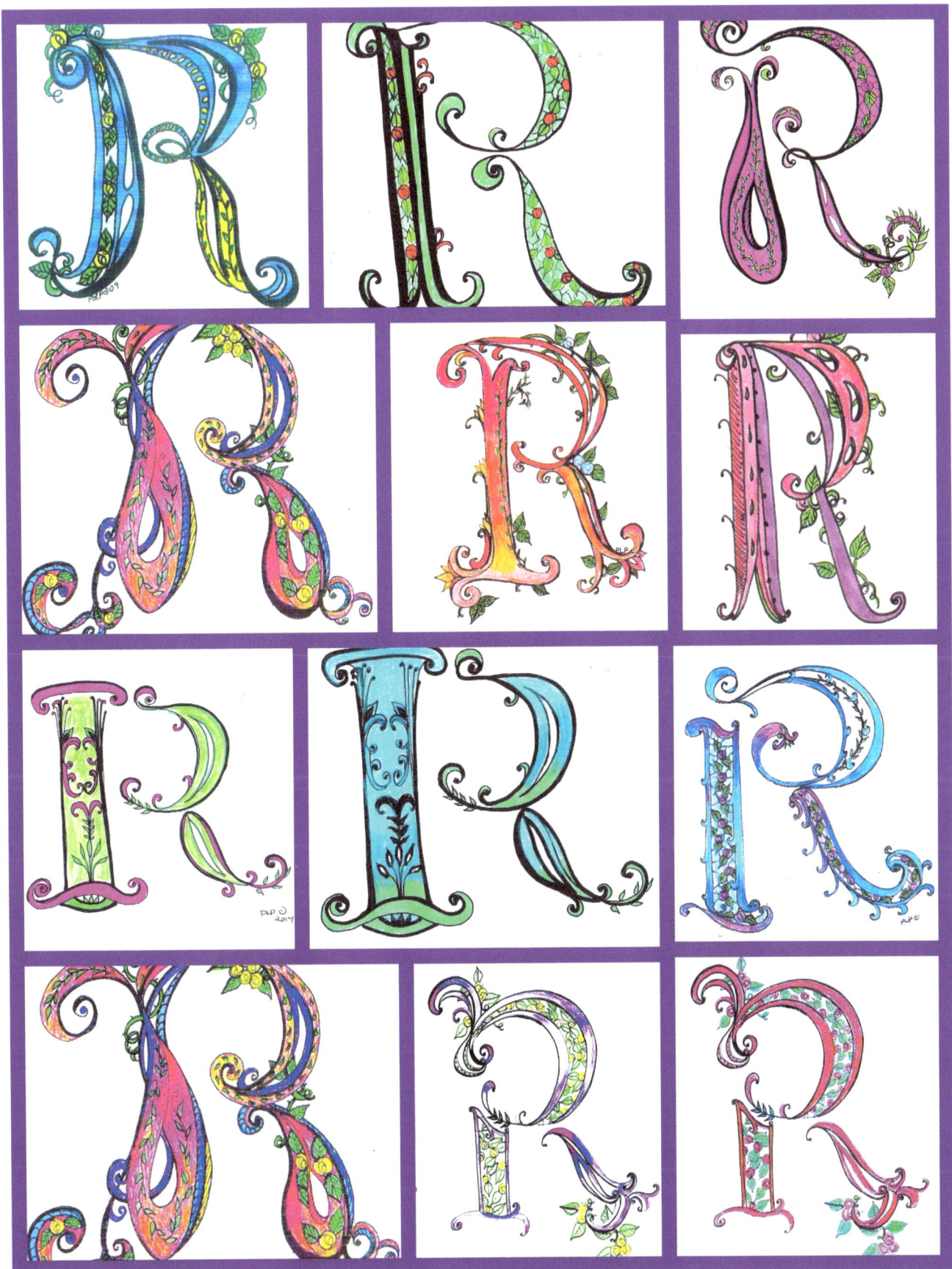

Sometimes Letter R likes to shine in the midnight.

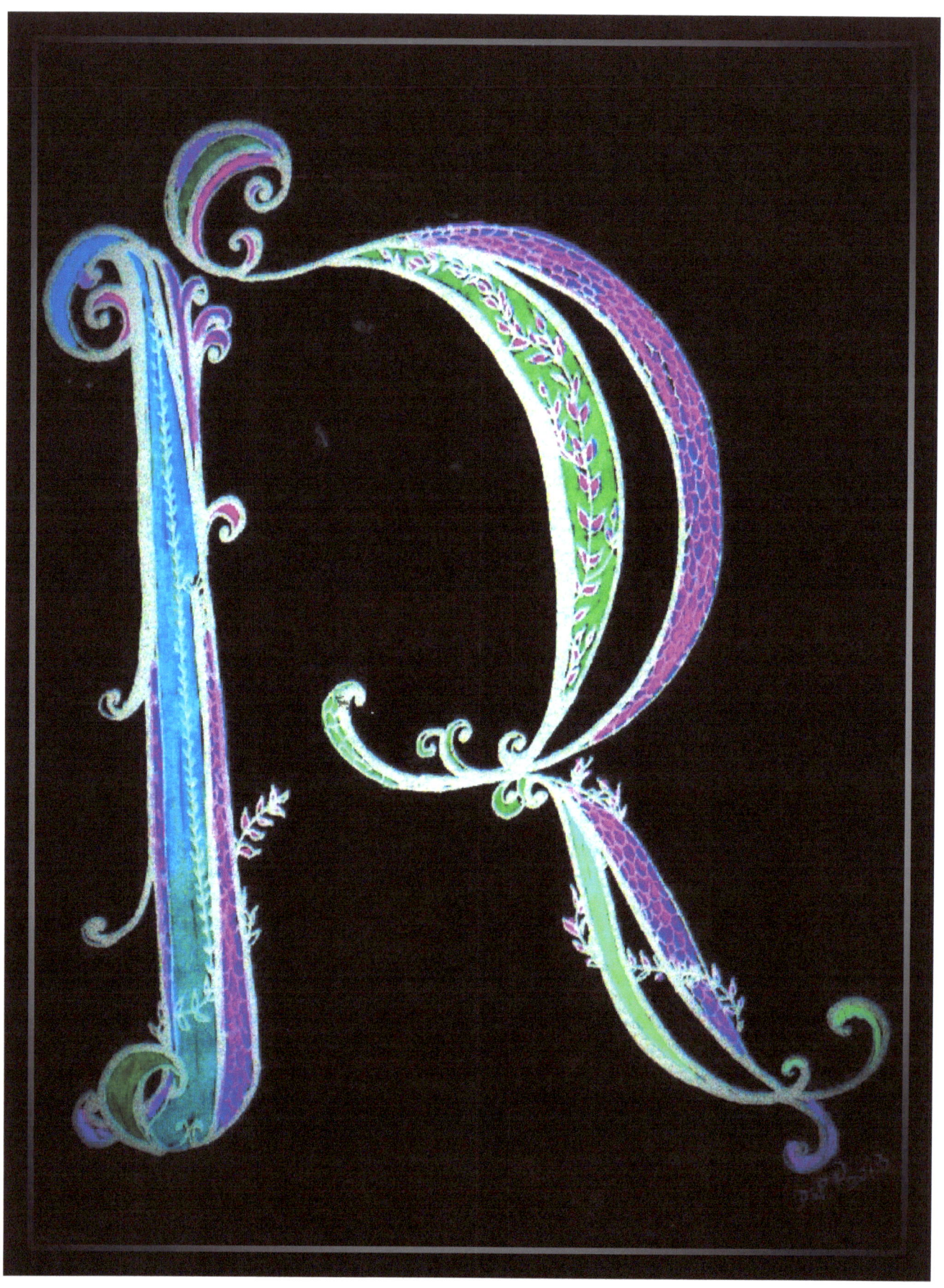

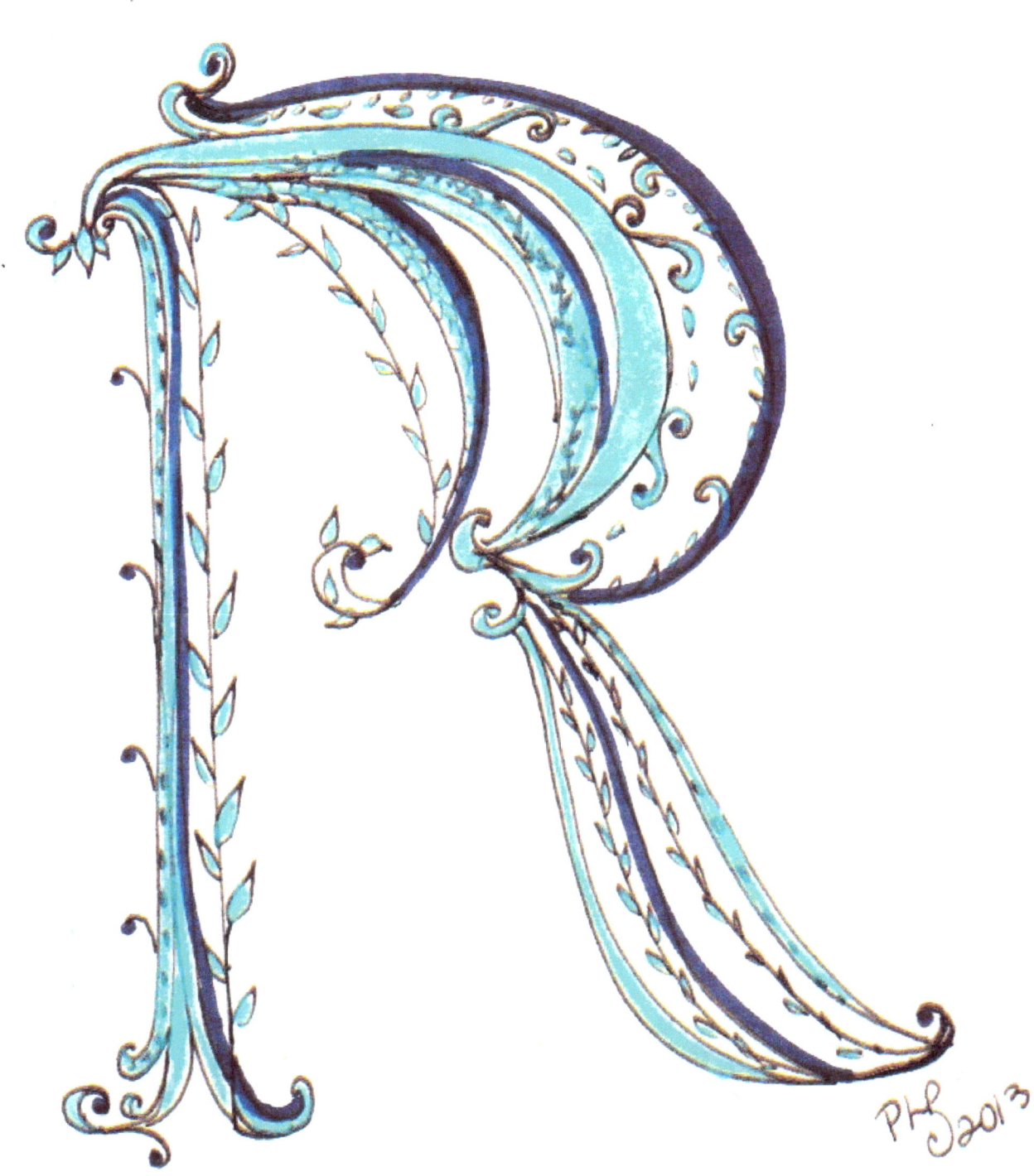

PHS 2013

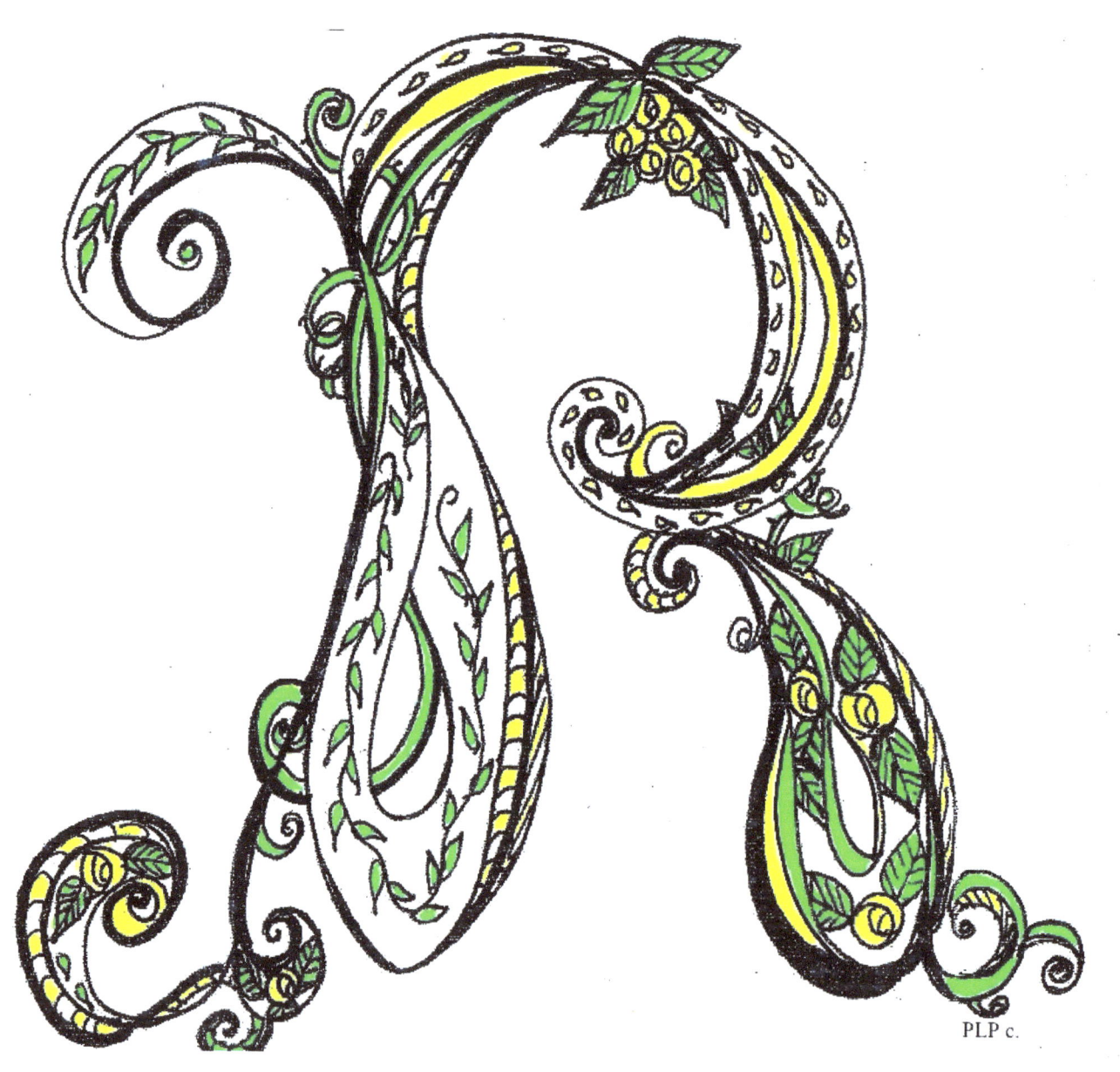

PLP c.

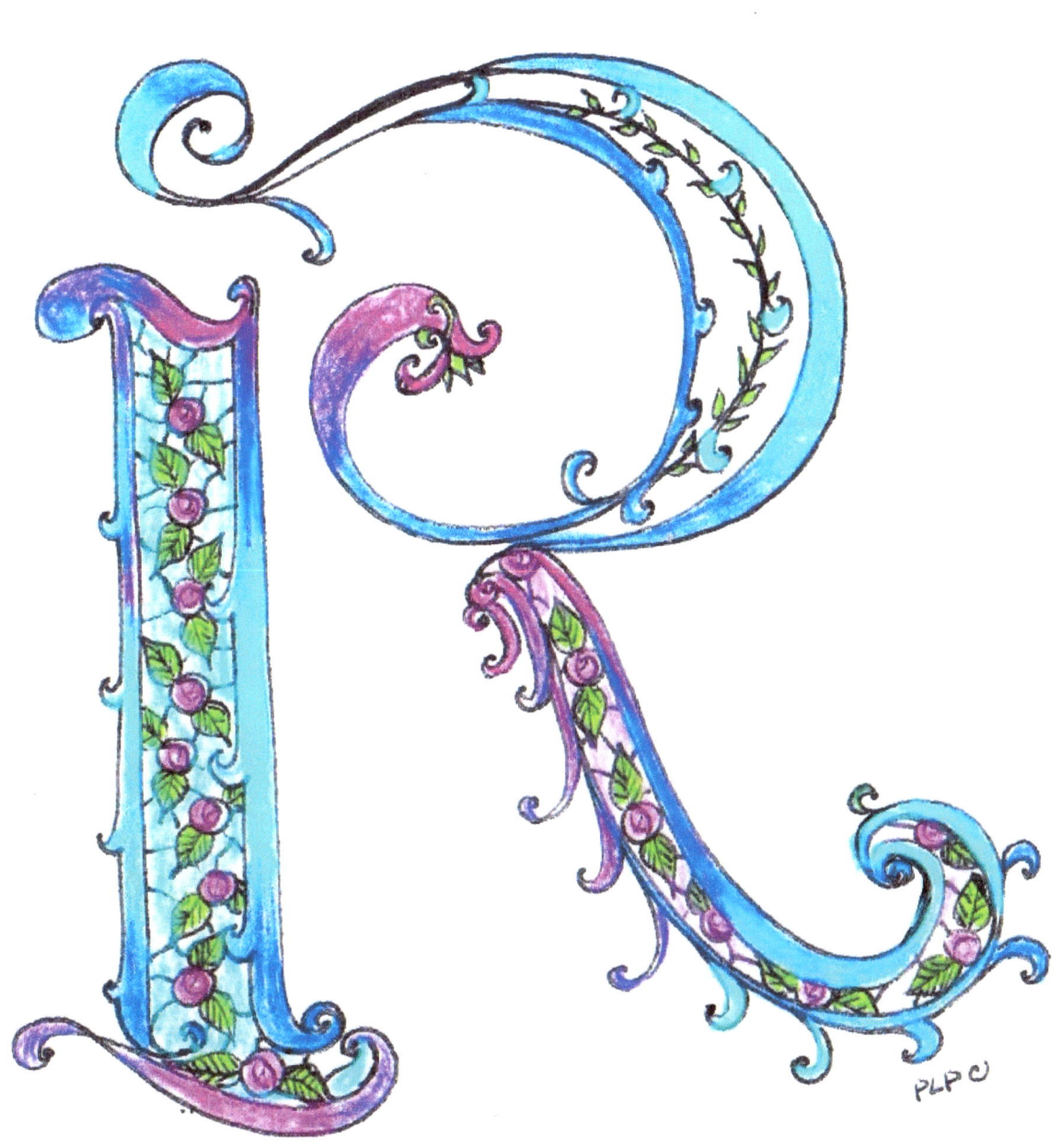

Thank you for visiting the letter R in this book. I hope you had fun choosing colors. If you are interested in other letter books they are either ready or coming out very soon. Write colored by at the bottom of your work and show it to others.

I hope you invent some further designs of letter R.

ENJOY!

Artist Peggy Louise Parrish

www.ingramcontent.com/pod-product-compliance
Lightning Source LLC
Chambersburg PA
CBHW051049180526
45172CB00002B/568